THE PHILLIP KEVEREN SERIES PIANO SOLO

CINEMA CLASSICS

CONTENTS

3	**Can You Feel the Love Tonight**	THE LION KING
8	**Cinema Paradiso**	CINEMA PARADISO
11	**Endless Love**	ENDLESS LOVE
14	**The Exodus Song**	EXODUS
22	**Forrest Gump—Main Title**	FORREST GUMP
17	**God Help the Outcasts**	THE HUNCHBACK OF NOTRE DAME
26	**Hands of Time**	BRIAN'S SONG
34	**Theme from "Lawrence of Arabia"**	LAWRENCE OF ARABIA
29	**My Heart Will Go On (Love Theme from 'Titanic')**	TITANIC
38	**Raiders March**	RAIDERS OF THE LOST ARK
42	**The Rainbow Connection**	THE MUPPET MOVIE
46	**Romeo and Juliet (Love Theme)**	ROMEO AND JULIET
49	**Somewhere, My Love**	DOCTOR ZHIVAGO
54	**Tears in Heaven**	RUSH
60	**Weep You No More Sad Fountains**	SENSE & SENSIBILITY

ISBN 978-0-634-01716-2

HAL•LEONARD®
CORPORATION
7777 W. BLUEMOUND RD. P.O. BOX 13819 MILWAUKEE, WI 53213

Visit Hal Leonard Online at
www.halleonard.com

PREFACE

The film music in this collection was not written originally for piano solo. Some of the compositions were orchestral in nature, designed to support and ignite the action on the screen. Others were songs with lyrics. My intent was to use "classical" writing techniques (thematic variation and development, etc.) to arrange each piece into a composition that felt as though it were first created for the piano. Although some of the settings do use devices from the classical repertoire (the Chopin-esque accompaniment in "Lawrence of Arabia," the Alberti bass in "Tears in Heaven"), that was not the driving force behind my approach.

Phillip Keveren
April 2000

BIOGRAPHY

Phillip Keveren, a multi-talented keyboard artist and composer, has composed original works in a variety of genres from piano solo to symphonic orchestra. Mr. Keveren gives frequent concerts and workshops for teachers and their students in the United States, Canada, Europe, and Asia. Mr. Keveren holds a B.M. in composition from California State University Northridge and a M.M. in composition from the University of Southern California.

CAN YOU FEEL THE LOVE TONIGHT

from Walt Disney Pictures' THE LION KING

Music by ELTON JOHN
Lyrics by TIM RICE

4

a tempo

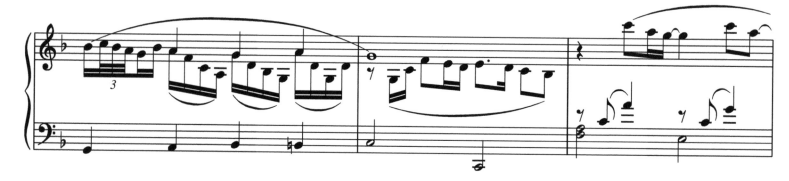

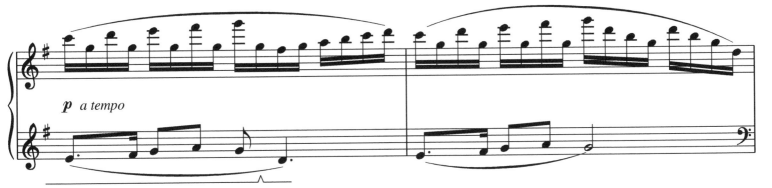

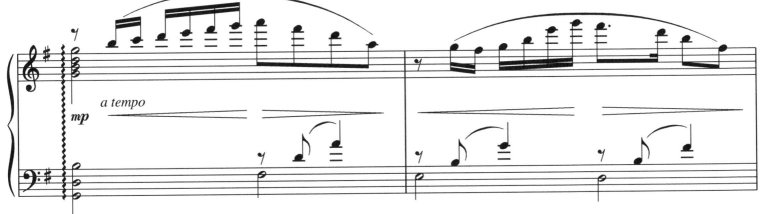

CINEMA PARADISO

from CINEMA PARADISO

Music by ENNIO MORRICONE

With grandeur

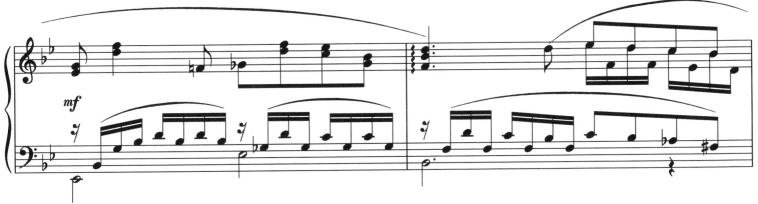

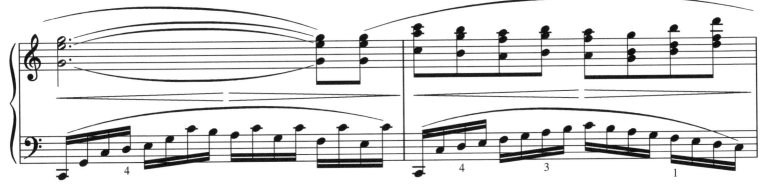

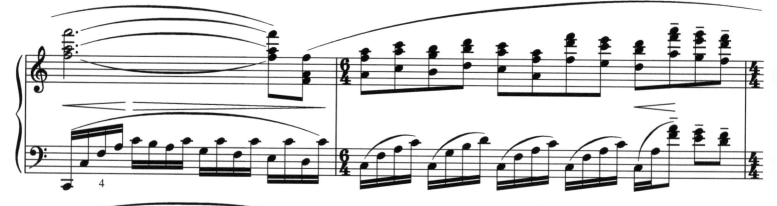

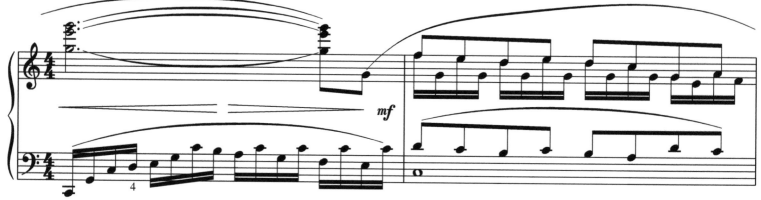

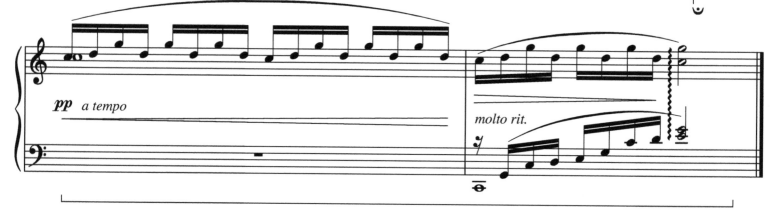

ENDLESS LOVE

from ENDLESS LOVE

Words and Music by
LIONEL RICHIE

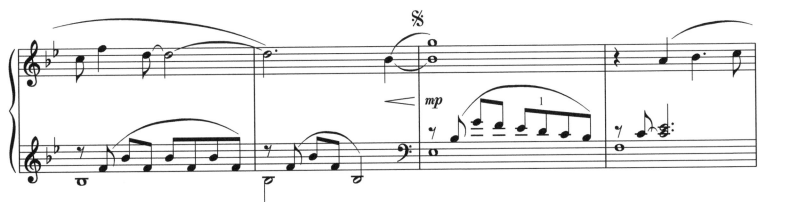

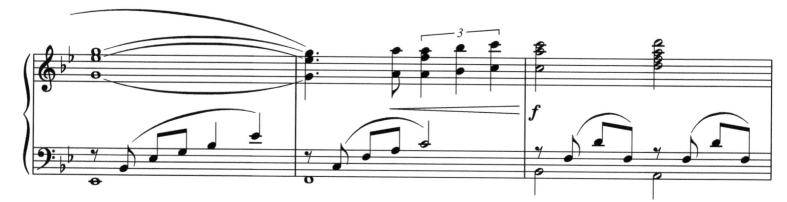

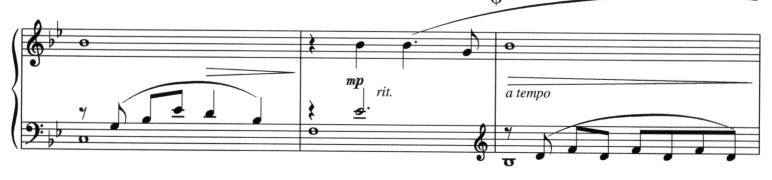

D.S. al Coda

CODA

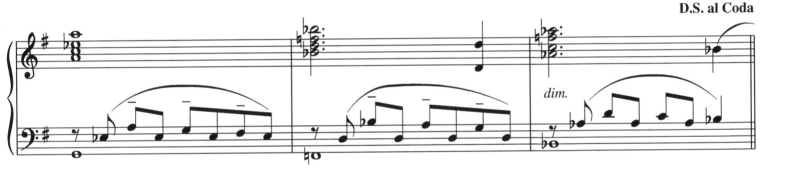

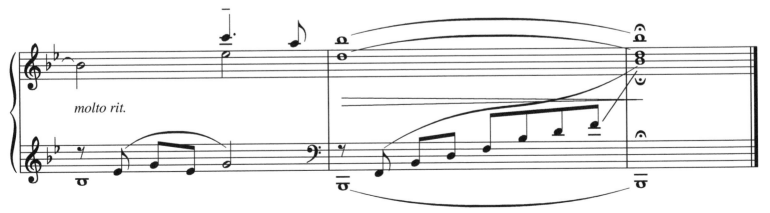

THE EXODUS SONG

from EXODUS

Words by PAT BOONE
Music by ERNEST GOLD

Very slow and solemn

poco a poco cresc.

Maestoso

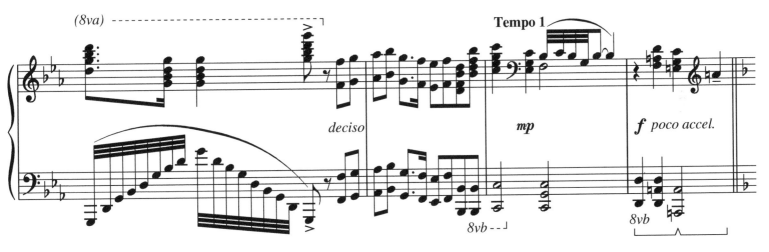

Flowing

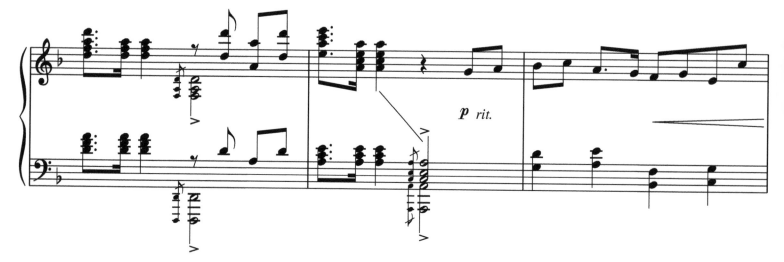

GOD HELP THE OUTCASTS

from Walt Disney's THE HUNCHBACK OF NOTRE DAME

Music by ALAN MENKEN
Lyrics by STEPHEN SCHWARTZ

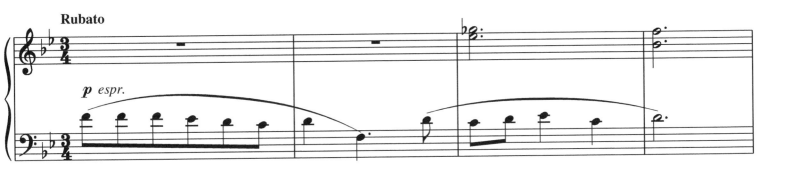

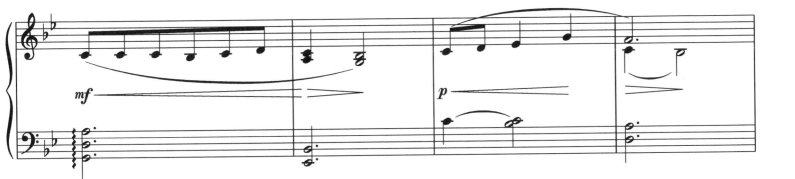

Passionately

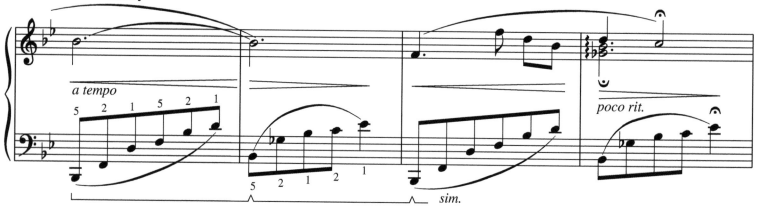

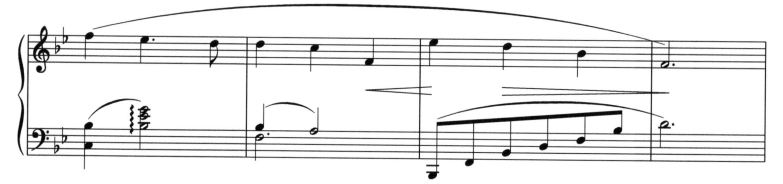

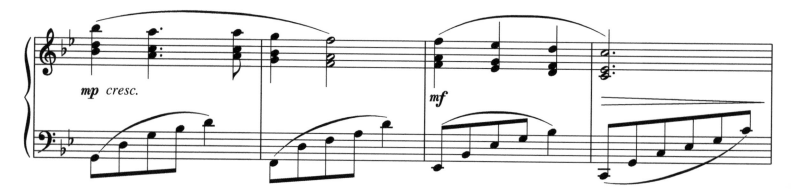

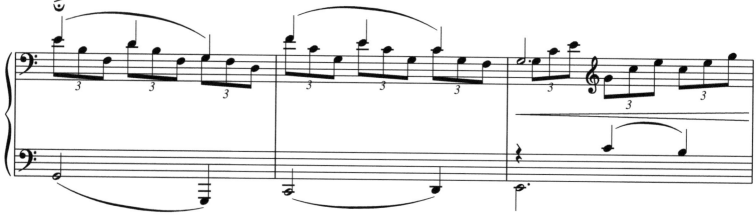

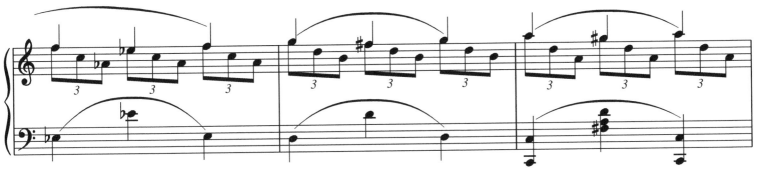

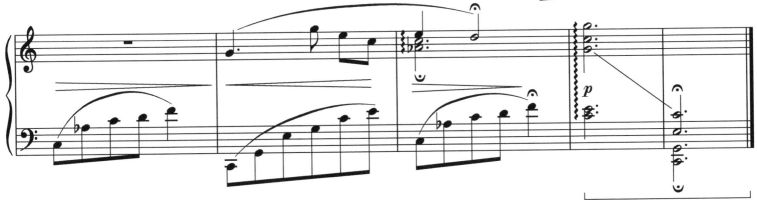

FOREST GUMP – MAIN TITLE
(FEATHER THEME)
from the Paramount Motion Picture FORREST GUMP

Music by ALAN SILVESTRI

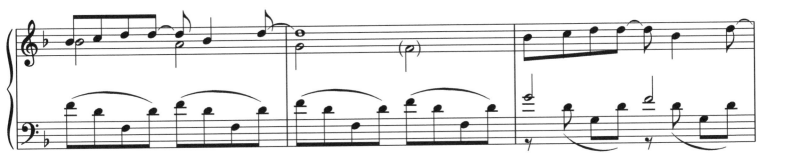

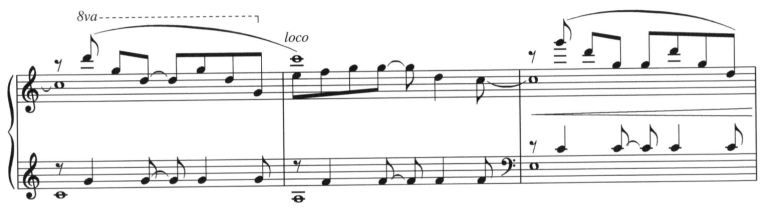

HANDS OF TIME

Theme from the Screen Gems Television Production BRIAN'S SONG

Words by ALAN BERGMAN and MARILYN BERGMAN
Music by MICHEL LEGRAND

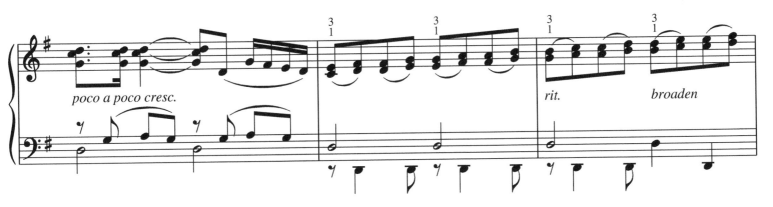

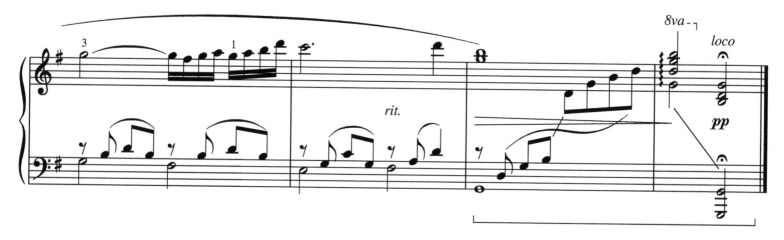

MY HEART WILL GO ON

(LOVE THEME FROM 'TITANIC')

from the Paramount and Twentieth Century Fox Motion Picture TITANIC

Music by JAMES HORNER
Lyric by WILL JENNINGS

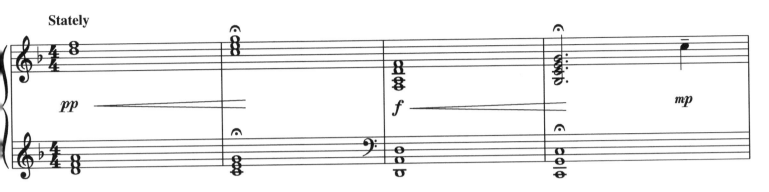

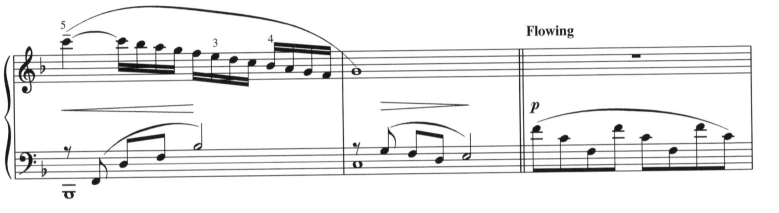

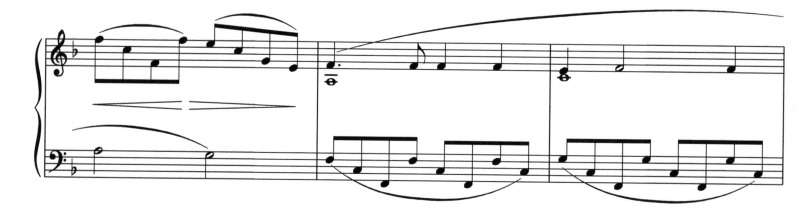

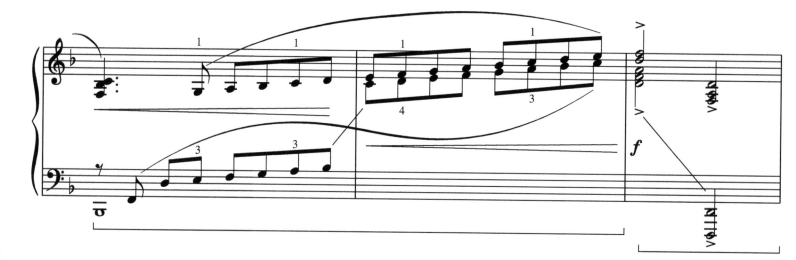

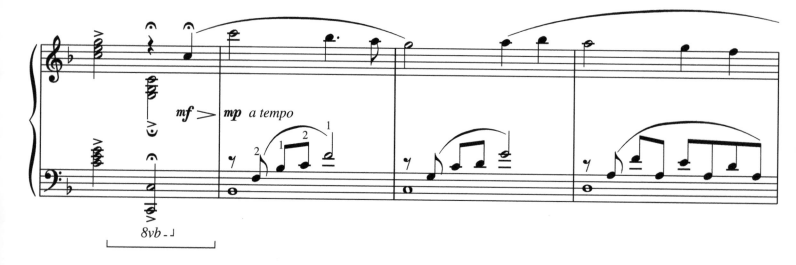

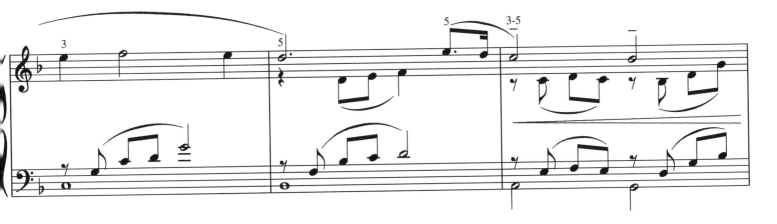

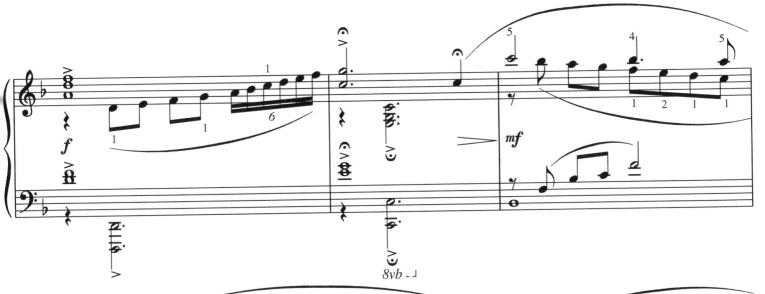

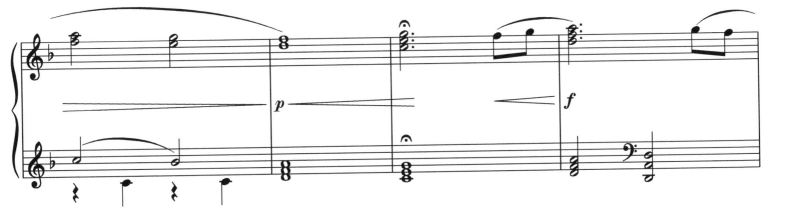

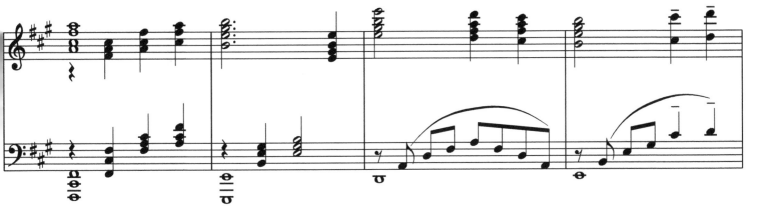

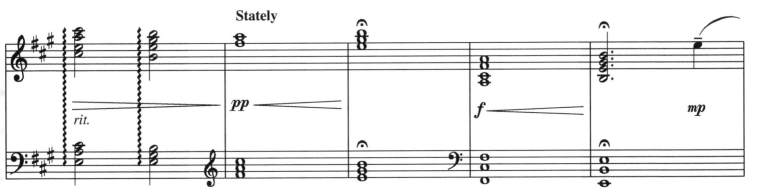

Stately

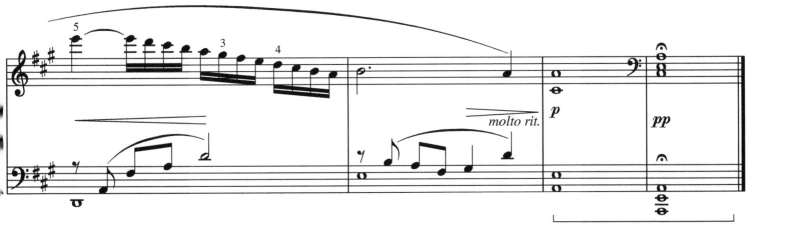

THEME FROM "LAWRENCE OF ARABIA"

from LAWRENCE OF ARABIA

By MAURICE JARRE

Passionately, quasi rubato

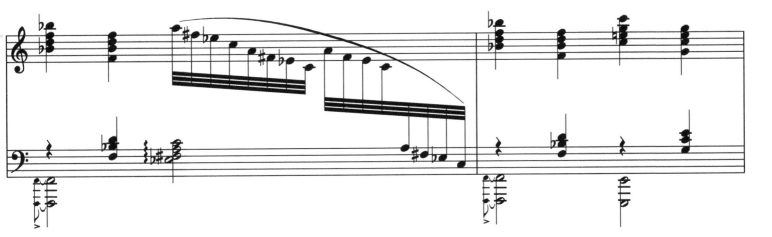

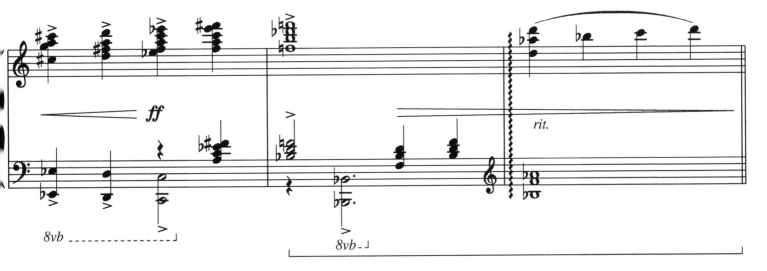

Più mosso

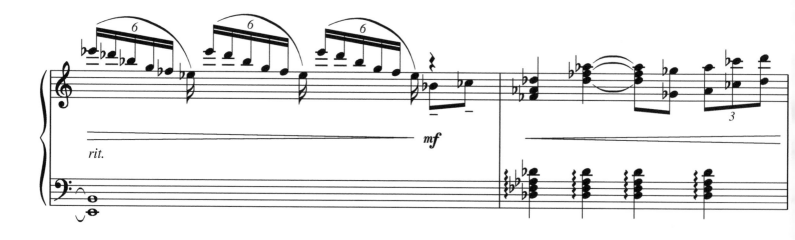

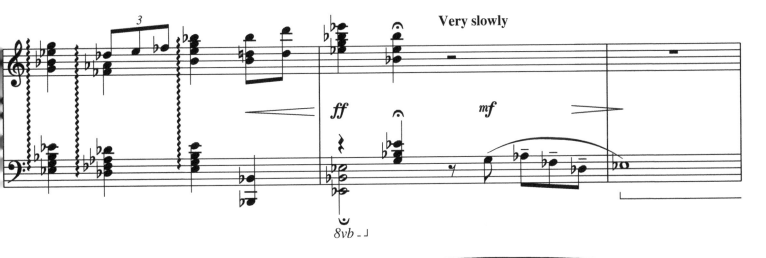

RAIDERS MARCH

from the Paramount Motion Picture RAIDERS OF THE LOST ARK
from the Paramount Motion Picture INDIANA JONES AND THE TEMPLE OF DOOM
from the Paramount Motion Picture INDIANA JONES AND THE LAST CRUSADE

Music by JOHN WILLIAMS

With animated precision

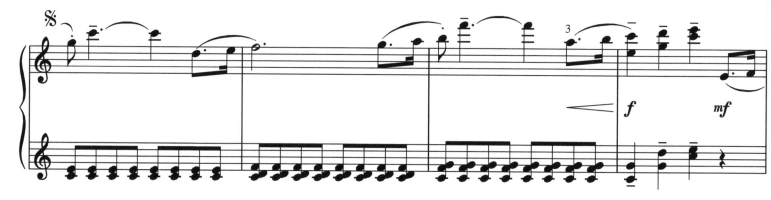

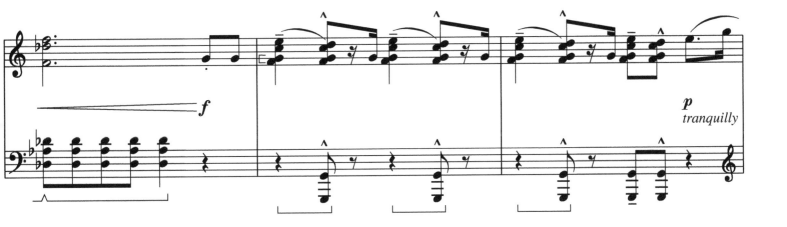

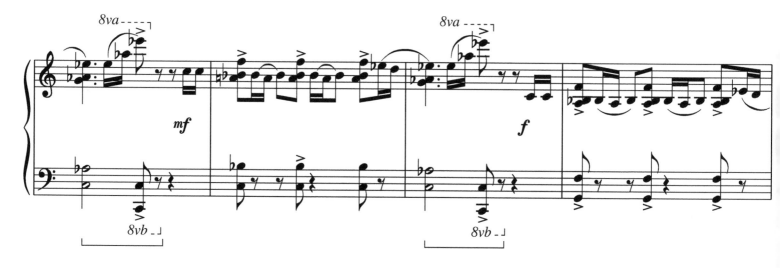

D.S. al Coda

THE RAINBOW CONNECTION

from THE MUPPET MOVIE

Words and Music by PAUL WILLIAMS
and KENNETH L. ASCHER

Smoothly gliding

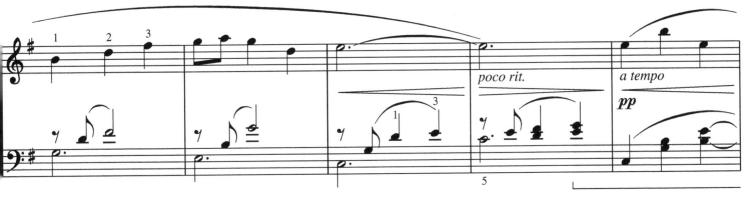

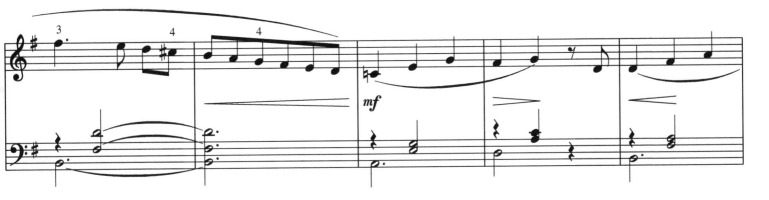

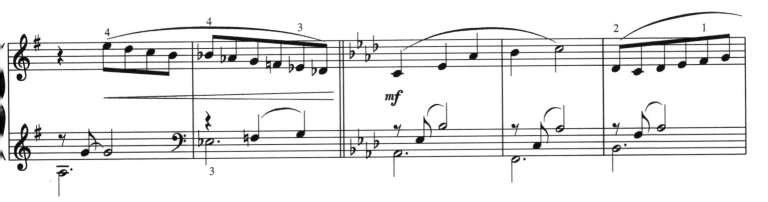

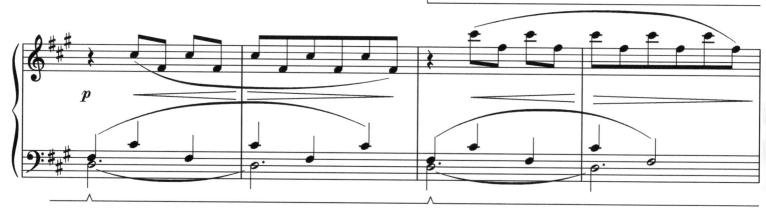

ROMEO AND JULIET
(LOVE THEME)
from the Paramount Picture ROMEO AND JULIET

By NINO ROTA

To Coda ⊕

D.S. al Coda

CODA

SOMEWHERE, MY LOVE
Lara's Theme from DOCTOR ZHIVAGO

Lyric by PAUL FRANCIS WEBSTER
Music by MAURICE JARRE

Bright Waltz

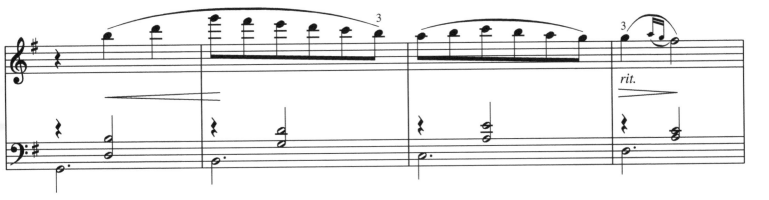

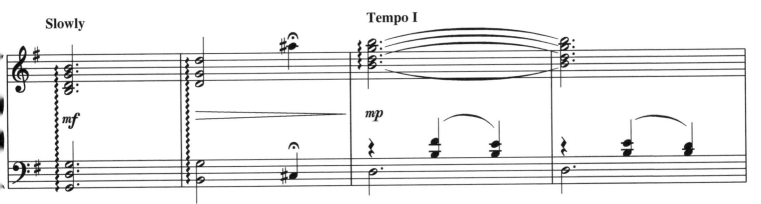

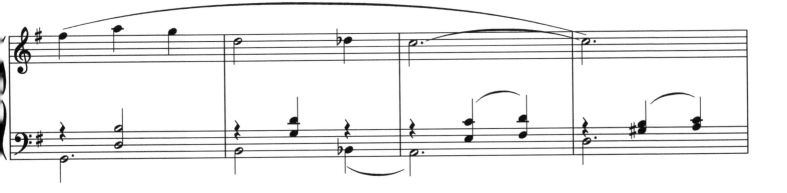

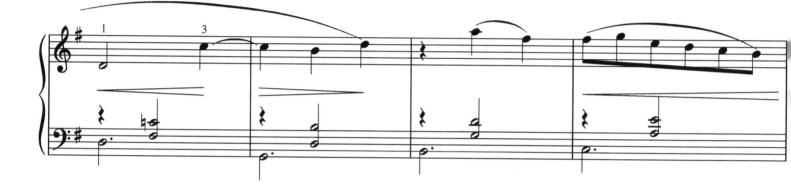

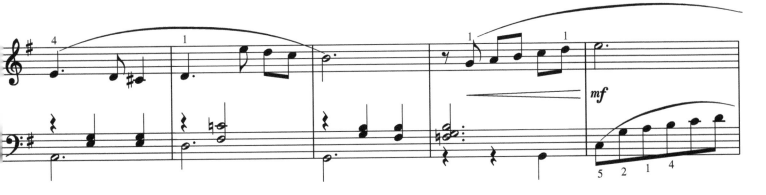

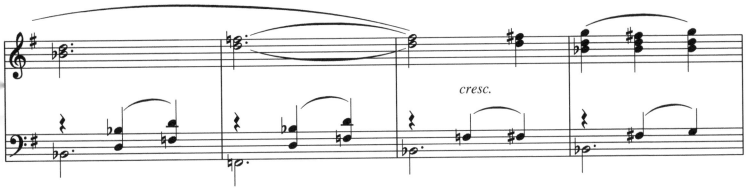

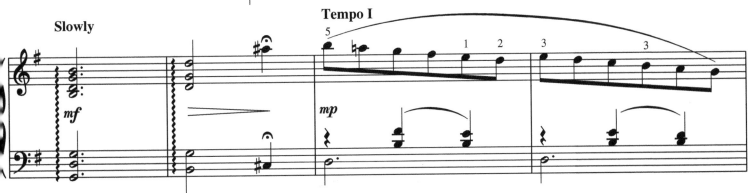

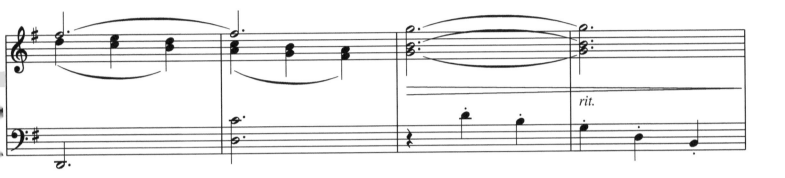

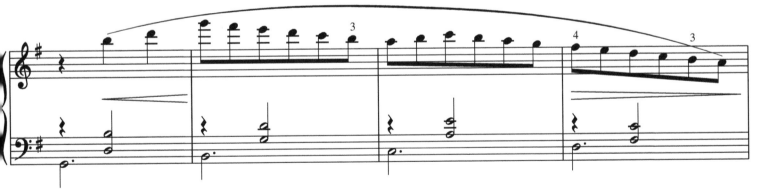

TEARS IN HEAVEN

featured in the Motion Picture RUSH

Words and Music by ERIC CLAPTON
and WILL JENNINGS

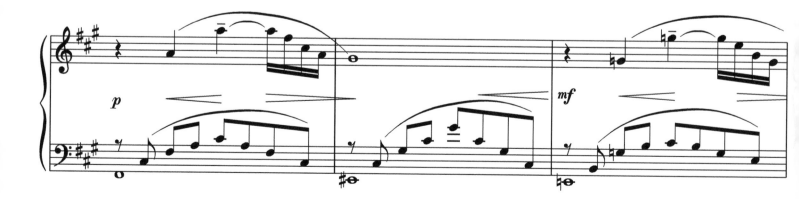

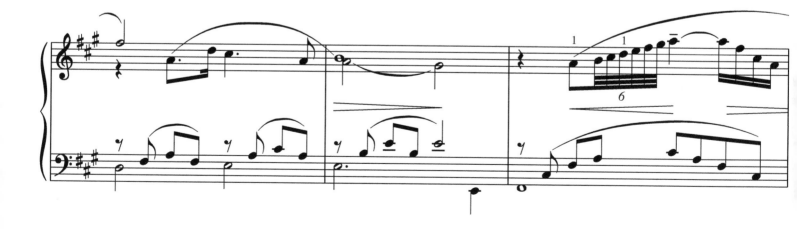

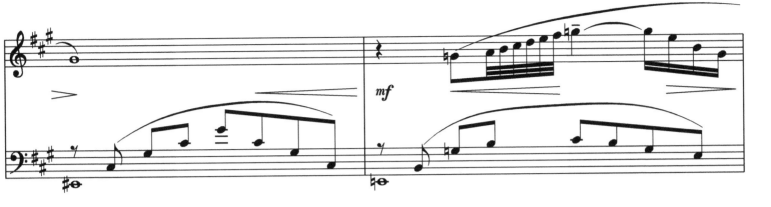

WEEP YOU NO MORE SAD FOUNTAINS

from SENSE & SENSIBILITY

By PATRICK DOYLE

Andante con moto

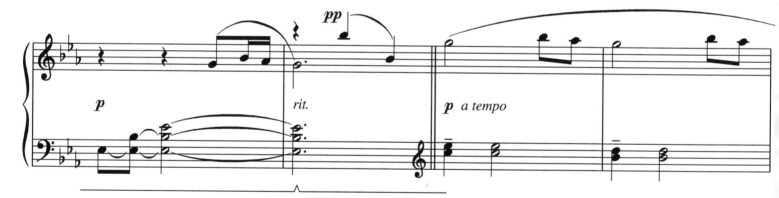

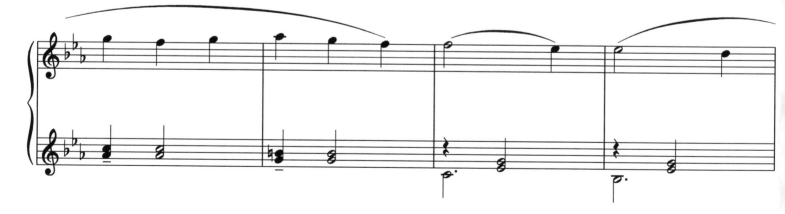

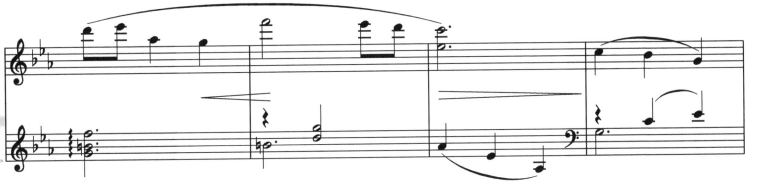

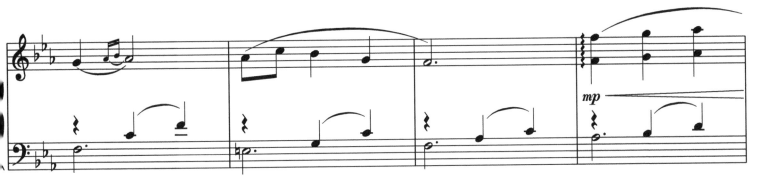

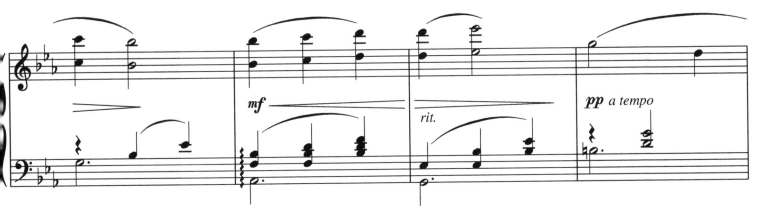

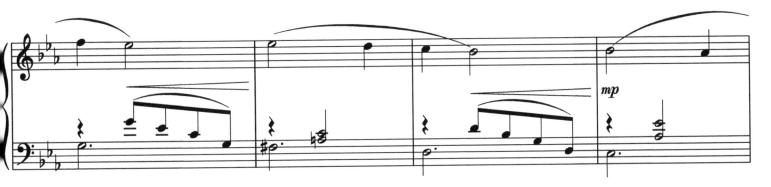

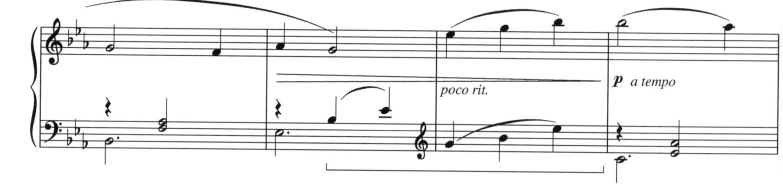

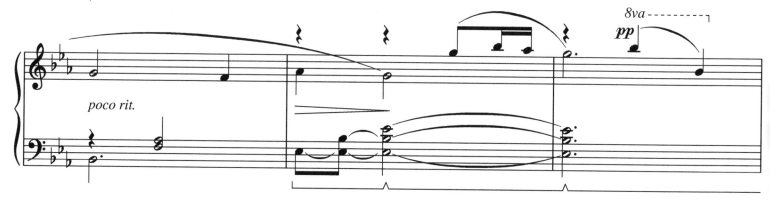

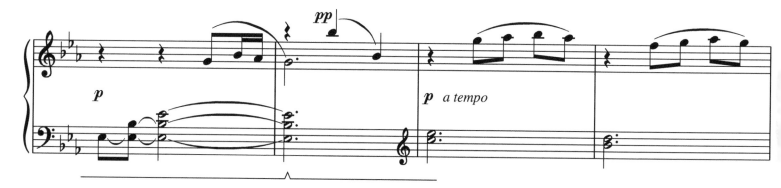

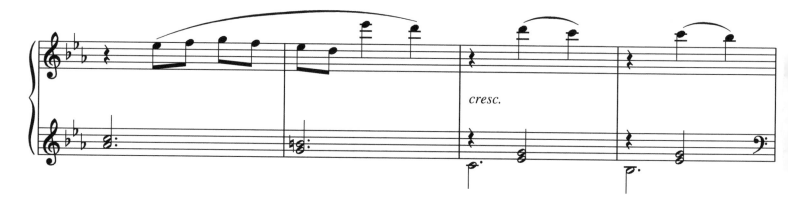

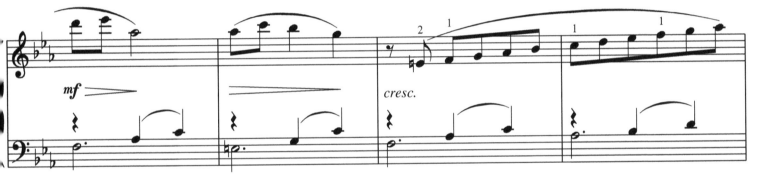

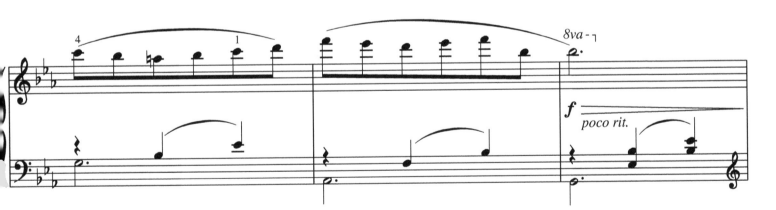

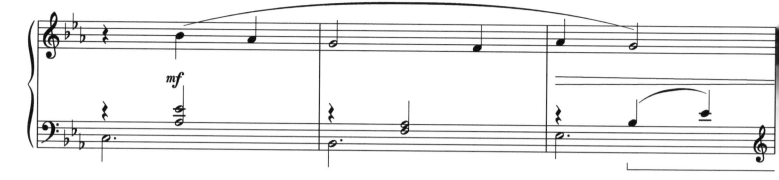

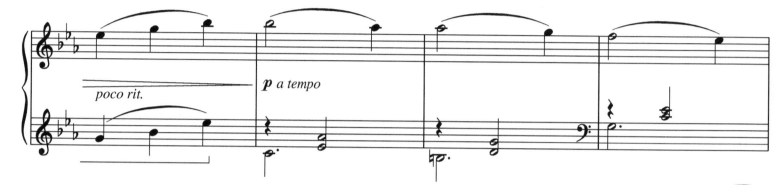

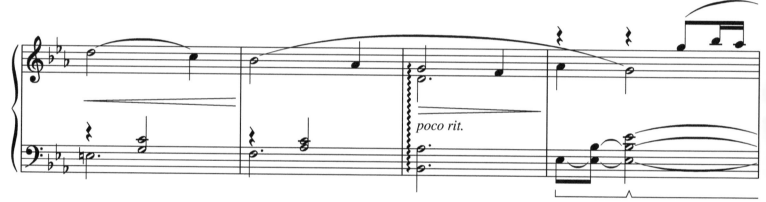

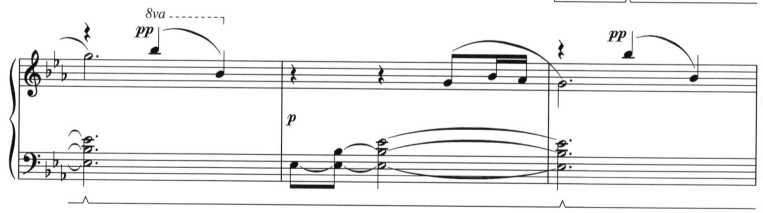

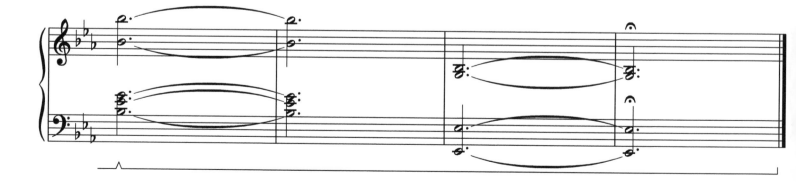